D1273098

LESSONS

LEARNED

IN

GOD'S

CLASSROOM

Patricia H. Storer

"You will call upon me
and come and pray to me,
and I will listen to you.
You will seek me and find me
when you seek me
with all your heart,"
declares the LORD.
                            ~Jeremiah 29:12,13

Contents

POEMS

PROLOGUE

All Christians could write about times when God broke through their cluttered lives to show them something special that was "just for them". I call these times "lessons" because I am learning something that God wants to teach me. Sometimes we give credit to luck, coincidence, chance, or even our own efforts for things that happen. When we do that, we are marked absent from class that day. We have missed the lesson.

If you have ever asked a group of people what God has done for them that week and they just stare back at you like a calf looking at a new gate, you realize that either they aren't being sensitive to the moving of the Holy Spirit in their lives or God isn't doing anything. We know that if you are a believer, God is always there and He is always working His good pleasure in your life every single day. So what's up?

If you are having delicate eye surgery or brain surgery you wouldn't want your surgeon to have calluses on his/her fingers, would you? This gives me a mental picture of the importance of not allowing calluses or buildup of worldly matters in your spirit that would keep you from receiving the lessons He has for you. We need to brush off those calluses and be aware of God at work in our lives.

Do you want to be like Christ in your daily life? How is that accomplished? A sculptor was once asked, "How do you make an angel?" He replied, "I just cut away anything that doesn't look like an angel." How does God make us like Christ?...well, you guessed it, He just cuts away anything that isn't like Christ. This process is sometimes painful, but God in His loving kindness does it in little daily lessons. The glory belongs to Him.....don't miss the lesson.

Do you have a "Gratitude Attitude"? Just start recounting the times when God has taught you a lesson. It won't be long before you are thanking God for all He's done and is doing in your life. Thank You, most gracious, Lord.

Disclaimer

The memories and perspectives are mine and may not agree with some of the people involved. One reason that I'm writing this now is I realize that at 79 years of age, my memories are growing dim and I want to record some of them before it's too late.

Perspectives are funny things....remember the story of the blind children who went to the zoo and they were allowed to touch an elephant? They were asked what an elephant was like....the one touching the leg said, "He's like a huge tree trunk." The one touching the elephant's tail said, "No, it's like a snake with a fuzzy part on the end." The one touching the trunk said, "No, you both are wrong; it's like a huge flexible pipe that spews water." All were right from their perspective.

Once I was leaving a church service and the lady next to me said, "That was the coldest service that I've ever been in." I thought that's strange because I felt that it was the most moving service that I had been to in a long time. What made the difference?

As you begin to read this little book…..please know that I'm not bragging on myself but I am bragging on our wonderful Lord who knows everything about us and who loves and cares about us anyway. Thank You, most gracious, Lord!!!!

~~~~~~

Thank you to my friends and family who took their time to review this book. You made the difference for me.

Also special thanks to Judy Kennamer, who shared her professional photographs on the covers…. You are definitely special.

Many thanks to Dr. Randy Stewart, published author of ten books, who took the time to lead me through the complicated publishing process. I literally couldn't have done it without you.

Most of all, thank you, Lord, for patiently teaching this stubborn student, who, when she is in her "right mind", wants to be more like Christ each day.

Lesson Title: Shooting Baskets

One of the earliest lessons that God taught me was painful, and this lesson still affects me today, some seventy years later.

I grew up in Mobile, Alabama. My Dad was one of thousands who came to Mobile at the end of WWII to get a job at the newly built Brookley Army Air Field. So many families came and overwhelmed the housing authority that the government quickly built a housing community. It was known as Birdville because all of the streets were named after birds. They also built a community center for the residents and their children.

My lesson began at the basketball courts there. It was just a game between local kids, and each team was built by the captains selecting team members. I was only 10 years old but I was excited to be selected by a teenage girl whom I greatly admired. The game started and I received the ball. I turned to face the basket and I gave it my best shot....I missed. That was bad enough, but the team captain whom I admired very much yelled, "You dummy, you haven't got brains God gave a goose."

At 10 years old I was totally humiliated...I wanted to fall into a hole. I don't remember much after that... I don't remember the girl's name or how she looked, but I can still hear her tone and inflection as she spoke those words that are burned into my brain like no others.

Many people would have just brushed them off and forgotten them, but God had a lesson in there for me to learn. In fact, several lessons came to my mind much later...

Lessons learned:

1. People aren't always kind.

2. Some people hurt you without even meaning to or knowing that they did.

3. What people say about you doesn't define who you really are.

4. Words have the power to crush someone's spirit or build them up.

God's instruction on how to put these lessons to use in our lives.

<u>Psalms 19:14</u> (NIV) – Let the words of my mouth, and the meditations of my heart, be acceptable in Thy sight, O Lord, my strength, and my redeemer.

<u>Proverbs 25:11</u> (NIV) – A word aptly spoken is like apples of gold in settings of silver.

<u>Proverbs 15:4</u> (NIV) – Gentle words bring life and health, a deceitful tongue crushes the spirit.

<u>Proverbs 18:21</u> (NIV) – Death and life are in the power of the tongue; and they that love it shall eat the fruit thereof.

Praying these words back to God.

My Lord and my God, may I always be aware of my words and how they can help people or hurt them. Sometimes I try to be funny and, in so doing, I may hurt others. Please forgive me, Lord, and put a watch over my lips. Amen!!!

Lesson Title – Good Gossip

"*Do you know what Peggy said about you?*" Usually what follows is a statement that you really don't want to hear. You could say, "No, I don't want to hear it because I don't care what she said." That could save you some heartache and embarrassment but somehow, because you are human, you say, "*What?*"

My best friend had brought the "gossip" to me, so when I said, "What?", expecting the worse, she told me what Peggy had said. She said "*I think Pat is the most sensitive and responsive person to the moving of the Holy Spirit that I've ever known.*" WOW!!! Now whether this was true or not, it impacted my life in the best of ways. It humbled me and made me want to be even more sensitive to the Holy Spirit. Good gossip does that!!

Our pastor had recently preached a message on gossip and the harmful effects it has on those involved....the gossiper and the one gossiped about. He shared verses like Proverbs 20:19, "A gossip goes around telling secrets, so don't hang around with chatterers" (NLT). He ended his sermon with a challenge to the congregation. "If you must gossip make it GOOD GOSSIP." I had never heard of such a thing---Good Gossip? What in the world is that? You thought all gossip had to be bad, didn't you? Now you know it doesn't have to be.

Lessons Learned:

1. Bad gossip discourages people.

2. Good gossip encourages people.

3. What we hear others say about us can make us bitter or better…It is our choice.

4. What we tell someone about others can hurt them or heal them.

5. Good friends always try to encourage us to be better Christians.

God's instruction on how to put these lessons to use in our lives.

Philippians 4:8 (NIV) – Finally brothers, whatever is true, whatever is noble, whatever is right, whatever is pure, whatever is lovely, whatever is admirable, if anything is excellent or praiseworthy, think about such things.

Proverbs 12:18 (NIV) – Reckless words pierce like a sword but the tongue of the wise brings healing.

Colossians 4:6 (NIV) – Let your conversation be always full of grace, seasoned with salt, so that you may know how to answer everyone.

Praying these words back to God.

Dear Lord, help me to watch what I say and how I say it. Forgive me when I have resorted to "bad gossip" and help me remember to share "good gossip" with others to encourage them in their walk with You. Amen!!!

Lesson Title:
Arguing with a Fence Post

My family likes to argue....You can call it intellectual disagreement or just a heated discussion of ideas, but whatever you call it my family loves to do it. We start off calmly stating our opinions and before you know it our voices are raised, our faces turn red, and anger is evident in our speech. It has been said many times about us, "They would argue with a fence post." Or, "When they argue, you might as well give in because they are like a turtle; once they clamp on in an argument, they won't turn loose until it thunders" (old wives' tale).

Once after church my husband and I were "discussing" a point the pastor made in his sermon. To us, we were having fun debating the issue, but to one of our sons it was disturbing since he had seldom heard us arguing. We didn't usually argue about real issues. He came to us and asked if we were getting a divorce. Until then I didn't realize how our habit of arguing affected our children.

There are subjects that, as adults, we have learned to avoid, i.e. politics and religion. I really don't like to argue...truth be told, I just want everyone to agree with me about everything, all the time......ha!!

God wanted to teach me a lesson about this, and He used Vidalia Onions to do it. My sister was visiting me from Georgia. We were in a restaurant and the subject of Vidalia Onions came up. We all know that Georgia is famous for them. Somewhere along the way I thought Vidalia Onions were purple. I proceeded to argue the point. We argued over it to the point we had to involve the waitress in our discussion before I would believe that Vidalia Onions were white not purple. Horrors! I was wrong!!!

I should have known better than to argue with a retired school teacher and long-term resident of Georgia about Vidalia Onions. God used that to show me some valuable lessons.

Lessons Learned:

1. I do not know everything.

2. God can take a person "down a peg or two" any way He wants to. He humbled me with an onion.

3. A contentious spirit is not a Christ-like attribute.

God's instruction on how to put these lessons to use in our lives:

Proverbs 21:23 (NIV) – He who guards his mouth and his tongue keeps himself from calamity.

Psalm 141:3 (NIV) – Set a guard over my mouth, O Lord. Keep watch over the door of my lips.

Proverbs 12:15 (NIV) – The way of a fool seems right to him, but a wise man listens to advice.

Romans 12:16a (NIV) – Live in harmony with one another.

Proverbs 11:2 (NIV) – When pride comes then comes disgrace, but with humility comes wisdom.

Praying these words back to God.

Dear Lord, thank You for teaching me Your ways. Help me to live according to Your guidance. Please stop me when I feel the urge to argue. Forgive me for my contentious spirit. Amen!!!

Lesson Title: A Lesson Missed

In God's classroom there was a day that I was absent from class and completely missed the lesson He wanted to teach me.

Years ago I worked at the Veterans Hospital in Battle Creek, Michigan. While employed there it was mandatory that all employees attend a class on how to do a breast self-exam. I never liked to do that because I thought I might find something. (I know, that's the object of it.)

Well, that day, I found a lump. The instructor checked it out, and she found it right away. She advised me to go to my doctor. I quickly went to my doctor, and he felt it too and ordered a scan. The scan revealed a suspicious spot and a biopsy was ordered. On the morning of the surgery, the surgical team from the Seventh Day Adventist Hospital gathered around my bed and prayed for me. The doctor had palpated the mass and drew a circle around it but when he made the cut to do the biopsy he couldn't find it. He made X-rays and took tissue from the area. When the lab results came in it was negative for any lump or cancerous tissue.

I left the hospital thinking, "Boy, I dodged the bullet that time." Pitiful, right? It was several years before I realized that I had been healed by God in answer to the prayers of His people. He healed me and I didn't acknowledge Him and what He had done. I didn't thank Him and I didn't give Him the glory for it. I totally missed the lesson that day.

Lessons Learned:

1. God hears and answers prayer for our good.

2. God forgives us when we sin by not thanking Him, giving Him the glory for what he does, or not acting on faith when we are troubled.

3. God heals according to His will.

4. God has plans for me and my future.

5. God is with us through our trials whether we are aware of it or not.

God's instruction on how to put these lessons to use in our lives:

James 5:15 (NIV) – And the prayer offered in faith will make a sick person well.

John 11:40 (NIV) – Jesus said to her, "Did I not tell you that if you believe you would see the glory of God?"

Matthew 18:19 (NIV) – "Again I say to you, if two of you agree on earth about anything they ask, it will be done for them by my Father in heaven."

Psalm 66:5 (NIV) – Come and see what God has done, how awesome His works in man's behalf.

Psalm 66:1 (NIV) – Shout with joy to God, all the earth! Sing the glory of His name; make His praise glorious! Say to God, "How awesome are Your deeds! So great is Your power that Your enemies cringe before You."

Praying those words back to God.

Thank You, Lord for acting on our behalf even when we miss the lesson. Thank You, for healing our hurts and providing prayer warriors to bear our requests to You. Thank You for healing this slow learner and showing me that it was from You. Amen!!!

Lesson Title: Unexpected

We were packed and loaded in the car to go to Maine for a family reunion. The only thing left to do was for me to go to the dermatologist so he could look at a mole on my leg and tell me that it was nothing to worry about. I've had many moles checked before and I never had anything to be concerned about. I didn't expect this one to be any different. When the doctor looked at it he immediately said, "This has all the signs of being a Melanoma Skin Cancer…I'm 99.9% sure it is one…..and I wouldn't allow any family member of mine to leave town without having it removed." So, my family was naturally disappointed to have to wait for the mole to be removed. It was sent to the lab with the results due in a couple of days.

You can imagine how "cheerful" I felt on the way to the reunion. I still had three children at home to raise. Since I always go to the worse-case scenario, I had my husband's next wife picked out. She was someone whom I knew would love and care for my children. Ha!!

After we returned home and we were at church, a man who was a new Christian came up to me and said that God had given him a scripture verse for me. WOW!!! I love it when that happens. It was <u>Romans 14:8.</u> "If we live, we live to the Lord; and if we die, we die to the Lord. So, whether we live or die, we belong to the Lord." That took the sting of death right out for me. The doctor called with the report from the lab....It was not a melanoma...not normal cells but not cancer either. I still have no fear of death or dying knowing that I belong to the Lord. Praise the Lord!!

Lessons Learned:

1. Worrying over things shows a lack of faith and doesn't help.

2. Only God knows the future.

3. I am in God's hands so I don't have to worry about living or dying. I belong to God.

4. God isn't through with me yet.

God's instruction on how to put these lessons to use in our lives:

James 5:14-15 (NIV) – Is any one of you sick? He should call the elders of the church to pray over him and anoint him with oil in the name of the Lord. And a prayer offered in faith will make a sick person well; the Lord will raise him up.

Matthew 6:27 (NIV) – Who of you by worrying can add a single hour to his life?

Jeremiah 29:11 (NIV) – For I know the plans I have for you, declares the Lord, plans to prosper you and not harm you, plans to give you a hope and a future.

Romans 14:8 (NIV) – If we live, we live to the Lord; and if we die, we die to the Lord. So, whether we live or die, we belong to the Lord.

Praying these words back to God.

Dear Father, forgive me for not trusting You with my life. I know worrying is a sin and please, forgive me, when I yield to that temptation. I need Your help to stop it. So please, help me to trust that You have my future in Your hands. I know You love me and I belong to You. I know You won't fail me. Amen!!!

Lesson Title: Along the Way

My youngest son was ready to start kindergarten, and since I worked full-time I needed a babysitter for the afternoons. A wonderful Christian lady named Ms. Sandy began keeping my son after school. One day he and I were out in our backyard, and he saw a special plant and began telling me how God made it so that, if you touched it, it would snap open and spread its seeds. He said Ms. Sandy told him about a lot of things that God made as they walked around her yard.

Many times after that my son told me about God and what Ms. Sandy said about Him. It dawned on me that Ms. Sandy taught my son more about God in those few hours she had him than I did in all of the rest of the time. She walked through her afternoon with my son telling him about God along the way.

God used her life and testimony to touch my son and me. I wonder if she even knew it.

Lessons Learned:

1. God uses ordinary Christians to help others.

2. Our daily walk with Christ can be a testimony for Him.

3. My daily walk with Christ needed to improve so I could be a better witness to my family.

4. People never know who is watching and listening to them.

God's instruction on how to put these lessons to use in our lives:

Matthew 5:16 (NIV) – In the same way, let your light shine before men, that they may see your deeds and praise your Father in heaven.

Titus 2:7 (NIV) – In everything set them an example by doing what is good. In your teaching show integrity, seriousness, and soundness of speech...

Colossians 1:28 (NIV) – We proclaim him, admonishing and teaching everyone with all wisdom, so that we may present everyone perfect in Christ.

Praying these words back to God.

Thank You, dear Lord, for teaching me through the example of others. Love in action is always good to see. Help me not to be selfish with my time. Help me to be sensitive to the needs of others and willing to give others the gift of time. Amen!!!

Lesson Title: God Speaks

Years ago I worked for the government in a warehouse-like room. Every employee was desk-to-desk, subjected to cigarette smoke, bad language, and noisy activities. Not the best of working conditions.....

One day I received a call from one of my sons who was in trouble at school. He had disobeyed his teacher's instructions and had been sent to the principal's office. He was telling me how he "didn't do it" and how unfair everyone was to him. I hung up the phone in disgust, grumbling under my breath. I complained to my co-worker that I was so tired of dealing with his problems.

My co-worker, who was not a Christian, but knew that I was, said, "Well, have you prayed about it?" What nerve she had to say such a thing!! She wasn't even a Christian. Could God be speaking through this lost woman to rebuke me for not having prayed about it? Oh, yes, He could and He did...He can do anything He wants...to anyone He wants.....anywhere He wants. He is the Almighty God and in control. God used my co-worker in this situation to teach me something very valuable.

Lessons Learned:

1. As Christians we are being watched to see if our "walk matches our talk."

2. God uses any means necessary to get through to us, even using a lost person's question.

3. Our faith in God to handle life's problems should be a testimony to a lost world.

God's instruction on how to put these lessons to use in our lives:

1 Peter 2:12 (NIV) – Live such good lives among the pagans that though they accuse you of doing wrong, they may see your good deeds and glorify God on the day He visits us.

Proverbs 19:20 (NIV) – Listen to advice and accept instruction, and in the end you will be wise.

<u>James 1:19</u> (NIV) – My dear brothers, take note of this: Everyone should be quick to listen, slow to speak, and slow to become angry.

Praying these words back to God.

Father, please forgive me when I fail to be a good testimony of how a Christ-follower deals with problems. Help me to realize that people watch my daily life to see if I am being faithful or not. I am grateful for Your forgiveness when I fail to do what is right. May my thoughts be ever on Your Almighty power to save. Amen!!!

Lesson Title: Testimony Disclaimer

If you have ever been on a mission trip to a country where the people don't speak English, you know the difficulties of working with an interpreter.

I went with a mission team from our church to Manaus, Brazil, where they speak Portuguese. My assignment on the first night was to share my Christian testimony with a small intercity congregation using an interpreter who was a college student from Belem. Another team member was a very nervous young man named Mark who was going to preach. When we arrived, I was overwhelmed by the friendliness of everyone. They were so grateful that we had "come so far" to minister to them, and they treated me like a celebrity...I was uncomfortable with that, so when I began my testimony, I wanted to assure the people there that I was just an average woman. I said that I was a common woman...a mother, a grandmother, and a daughter......When I finished, I sat down and the pastor immediately stood up and gave a disclaimer to my testimony concerning a mistranslation by the interpreter. Evidently the words "common woman" were translated as "a woman of the streets."

From that point on, everywhere I went, I was inundated by women wanting me to sign their Bibles, to meet their families, and their friends. Since I didn't speak Portuguese, I always felt like they were introducing me as a "sinful woman of the streets miraculously saved by God from a life of great sin."

Each time I just smiled at them knowing that even though I had never been a "woman of the streets" I truly was "a sinful woman saved by God's matchless grace." The young preacher's efforts were also rewarded that night when he heard that two people were saved after he preached. Thank You, Jesus, for using us even in our weakness!!!

Lessons Learned:

1. Obedience to God sometimes places you in strange places among strange people who need to know the Lord.

2. God can use even our "mistakes" for His glory.

3. God gives us the grace not to be thrown when embarrassing things happen.

4. You can witness to people about God's love without speaking their language – with smiles, hugs, and kindness.

5. God gives you a love for people around the world that you don't even know.

6. God rewards our efforts when we step out in faith even if we are nervous or afraid.

God's instruction on how to put these lessons to use in our lives:

1 Peter 4:14 (NIV) – If you are insulted because of the name of Christ, you are blessed, for the Spirit of glory and of God rests on you.

2 Corinthians 12:9-10 (NIV) – But He said to me, "My grace is sufficient for you, for My power is made perfect in weakness." Therefore I will boast all the more, gladly about my weaknesses so that Christ's power may rest on me. That is why, for Christ's sake I delight in weakness, in insults, in hardships, in persecution, in difficulties. For when I am weak, then I am strong.

John 3:16 (NIV) – For God so loved the world that He gave His one and only Son, that whoever believes in Him shall not perish but have eternal life.

Matthew 28:19 (NIV) – Therefore, go and make disciples of all nations, baptizing them in the name of the Father and of the Son and of the Holy Spirit, and teaching them to obey everything I have commanded you; and surely I am with you always, to the very end of the age.

Praying these words back to God.

Almighty God, help me to see people through Your eyes. You loved and died for each one. Help me to see that no one is beyond Your saving grace. Increase my faith in You to save a lost and dying world. Thank You for allowing us be a part of Your plan. Amen!!!

Lesson Title: Mean as a Snake

Whether we are aware of it at the time or not, people are looking at us as Christians to see if our faith is real. Perhaps there should be a sign on our lives saying, "WARNING: YOU ARE BEING WATCHED". If you are a Christian, I think people are watching you so they can see if you are doing something that doesn't match up with what you say you believe. They delight in "catching you" in an action that doesn't line up, because, in their eyes, it vindicates their unbelief.

I worked with a lady claiming to be a Christian who had her own office. It was decorated with Christian sayings and Bible verses all over the walls. But she was a mean-spirited woman, judging people and saying unkind things to most everyone. Many of her co-workers had noticed. After one particularly tense encounter with her boss, her boss came to me said, "I don't care how many Bible verses she has pinned on her walls, she's still mean as a snake."

People watching you can be a good and an encouraging thing. Once I was working at my desk and I overheard two women on the other side of the filing cabinets talking about a particularly obnoxious man. After talking about him for a while one said, "I bet even Pat can't come up with something good to say about him." Until then, I had never realized that when someone said something bad about someone, I would try to think of something good to say about them. I didn't even know I was doing that. Good or not, God had a lesson for me in that. I was being watched and not just by my co-workers but by God Himself. Our children are taught that lesson at an early age with the little song, "Be careful little hands what you do, for the Father up above is looking down in love, so be careful little hands what you do."

Lessons Learned:

1. People are watching what we say and do, as a representative of Christ.

2. It is encouraging when people say something good about you.

3. Even as a Christian, we can be a hypocrite, if our actions aren't Christ-like.

God's instruction on how to put these lessons to use in our lives:

<u>Matthew 15:7-9</u> (NIV) – You hypocrites! Isaiah was right when he prophesied about you: "These people honor Me with their lips, but their hearts are far from Me. They worship Me in vain; their teachings are but rules taught by men."

<u>James 1:26</u> (NIV) – If anyone considers himself religious and yet does not keep a tight rein on his tongue, he deceives himself and his religion is worthless.

<u>1 John 4:20</u> (NIV) – If anyone says, "I love God," yet hates his brother, he is a liar. For anyone who does not love his brother, whom he has seen, cannot love God, whom he has not seen.

Praying these words back to God.

Dear Jesus, I pray that You will help me live my life in a way that pleases You. I don't want to be a hypocrite... help me to be real in my daily life. Thank You for saving me and allowing me to be a part of Your Kingdom's work. Amen!!!

Lesson Title: Down in the Dumps

Ever feel "down in the dumps"? You feel discouraged, unloved, lonely, useless, and all around miserable. If you have, God cares about that because when you are down in the dumps, you are virtually out of commission as far as serving God goes. Being a Christian doesn't mean every day will be all sunshine and roses. There will be times that are downright depressing. But God never allows us to stay there for very long.

An evangelist asked a woman how she was doing and she said, "Okay, under the circumstances." He replied, "What are you doing under there?" Good question!!

Once I was feeling a bit useless, that my life didn't matter much. I had just gotten a computer and was online. I received a message from someone whose name I didn't recognize, saying, "Are you the Ms. Pat that used to be the youth leader in San Antonio? If so, I want to thank you for crying and praying over us. I still have the Bible that you gave me." God reached down in His love and touched my heart through this young man's encouraging message. To be honest, I had trouble remembering who this young man was, but God knew I needed encouragement and He used someone I hadn't seen in over 40 years to do it. Out of the blue, from someone I couldn't remember, God told me that my life had helped someone and that He wanted me to continue trying to help others. I'll never forget this young man because his loving encouragement helped me climb out of the dumps into God's glorious sunshine.

We have so much to be thankful for....we just get distracted sometimes and need to be reminded.

Lessons Learned:

1. God is amazing and surprises us all the time.

2. God uses anyone He wants to encourage us.

3. We influence others sometimes without even realizing it.

4. God won't allow His children to be down and out of commission for very long.

5. He renews us in our spirits so we can help others who are also in the dump.

God's instruction on how to put these lessons to use in our lives:

<u>Psalm 51:12</u> (NIV) – Restore to me the joy of Your salvation and grant me a willing spirit to sustain me.

<u>Psalm 51:10</u> (NIV) – Create in me a pure heart, O God, and renew a steadfast spirit within me.

<u>Isaiah 55:11</u> (NIV) – So is My word that goes out from My mouth: It will not return to Me empty, but will accomplish what I desire and achieve the purpose for which I sent it.

<u>Job 16:5</u> (NIV) – But My mouth would encourage you; comfort from My lips would bring you relief.

<u>1 Thessalonians 5:11</u> (NIV) – Therefore encourage one another and build each other up, just as in fact you are doing.

<u>James 1:2-6</u> (NIV) – Consider it pure joy, my brothers, whenever you face trials of many kinds, because you know that the testing of your faith develops perseverance. Perseverance must finish its work so that you may be mature and complete, not lacking anything.

<u>2 Corinthians 1:3-4</u> (NIV) – Praise be to the God and Father of our Lord Jesus Christ, the Father of compassion and the God of all comfort, who comforts us in all our troubles, so that we can comfort those in any trouble with the comfort we ourselves have received from God.

Praying these words back to God.

Oh Lord, My God. Thank You for loving me even when I lack faith to trust You with my troubles. Help me to turn to You when I feel down and out. Help me to remember to be grateful for all You do for me. Give me the grace to be willing to help others. Amen!!   *!*

Lesson Title:
I Can't...Never Could (Part 1)

"Lord, I can't do that. I've never done anything like that before. I wouldn't know where to start."

When God wants me to do something out of my comfort zone, I've always tried to give an excuse to Him and wiggle out of it. But, in the end, I surrender to what He wants because He won't leave me alone about it; and, if I'm being truthful, I know a blessing is waiting for me when I do.

That's what happened when God wanted me to go to The Village, a low-income housing project, to help the women there. Nearly every day there was news on TV and in the newspapers about rapes, drug use, beatings, assaults, and even murders. I didn't want to go, and I couldn't get any other ladies from my church who would commit to going with me.

When I said, "I can't do it," God reminded me that "I can do all things through Christ who strengthens me" (Philippians 4:13).

When I said, "I've never done anything like that before," God said, "Commit to the Lord whatever you do, and your plans will succeed" (Proverbs 16:3).

When I said, "I didn't know where to start," He said, "Call to me and I will answer you and tell you great and unsearchable things you do not know" (Jeremiah 33:3).

After surrendering to God's call to The Village, I felt I should go to the manager's office. I stepped inside and I literally didn't know what to say, other than the truth of the matter: "I'm here because God told me to come." The lady manager was a committed Christian and she began to cry. "I've been praying that God would send someone who would tell our ladies that God loves them. So, what do 'we' do next?"

All of a sudden I wasn't alone in this. God had provided a partner to help me. She suggested a survey to see what the women would be interested in doing. So, a survey was done and plans were made to begin an Arts and Crafts Class. I didn't know much about arts and crafts. I wanted to do a Bible Study but only one had marked on the survey that they were interested in having one. I couldn't get anyone else from my church to go with me to help with the class because they were afraid of the many crimes committed there. But when I finally obeyed God and said that I would go, I never had a single moment's fear. God is good and He provides all we need to get the job done. It was a joy to see how God was working things out.

Lessons Learned:

1. God speaks to us through different means when He has a job for us to do.

2. God is persistent in going after us to do His will.

3. God loves people who we consider "unlovable".

4. God has a plan to see that all are invited to accept His salvation.

5. Joy abounds when we obey Him.

6. It's exciting to see God at work in our daily lives.

God's instruction on how to put these lessons to use in our lives:

Romans 5:8 (NIV) – But God demonstrates His own love for us in this: While we were still sinners, Christ died for us.

Isaiah 14:24 (NIV) – The Lord Almighty has sworn, "Surely, as I have planned, so it will be, as I have purposed, so it will stand."

Psalm 37:23-24 (NIV) – If the Lord delights in a man's way He makes his steps firm; though he stumble, he will not fall for the Lord upholds him with His hand.

2 Timothy 1:7 (KJV) – For God hath not given us the spirit of fear; but of power, and of love, and of a sound mind.

Praying these words back to God.

Heavenly Father, thank You for calling me to work at The Village. It was scary at first but You gave me the courage to attempt it. You blessed me in so many ways through helping these people. You gave me a love for them that was supernatural. It was from You. Thank You. Amen!!!

Lesson Title: What Next? (Part 2)

The ministry at The Village began when a survey was done and the women wanted to do an Arts and Crafts Class so they could make some Christmas ornaments and gifts. On the first night of the class, I told those gathered that I was there because God told me to come...I'm sure some thought I was just another "religious fanatic" come to tell them they were all going to hell. I also told them that I wasn't going to try to pressure them in any way to turn to my religion but I was there if they needed me.

After several weeks of making Christmas gifts, one lady asked if I had seen the newspaper article about a lady resident's boyfriend who had been arrested for sexually abusing her two children. I said that I had. The Mother had attended our class but wasn't there that night. The lady asked if we could pray for her...and, of course, I said yes. The next week another member of our class asked if we could pray for her because she was having an interview the next day and she really needed the job. That began a wonderful time of God moving in the hearts of the women of The Village to reach out to Him for help. He was definitely doing the "leading" and I was just trying to keep up.

Lessons Learned:

1. God has His plans and we just need to follow His leading.

2. We don't have to fear what happens next when God is in control.

3. Even lost people know that God is the answer to their troubles.

4. If we say "no" to God's leading, we miss the blessings.

God's instruction on how to put these lessons to use in our lives:

Matthew 5:16 (NIV) – In the same way, let your light shine before men, that they may see your good deeds and praise your Father in heaven.

James 4:17 (NIV) – Anyone, then, who knows the good he ought to do and doesn't do it, sins.

Ephesians 2:10 (NIV) – For we are God's workmanship, created in Christ Jesus to do good works, which God prepared in advance for us to do.

Praying these words back to God.

Heavenly Father, I pray that You will continue to be patient with me, teaching me to obey You in my daily life. Show me how to live here. Help me to be willing to give of myself and my time so others can come to know You as their Savior and Lord. Amen!!!

Lesson Title: Scared to Death

San Antonio is an exciting city to live in. As Christians we had many opportunities to witness and share God's love with others.

Our church's youth group was invited to participate in a city-wide evangelism effort at the malls. Our group was assigned one of the smaller neighborhood malls. We gathered in the church parking lot to pray before we went. Truthfully, I had never done this before and it was hard to tell the youth what to do and how to do it since I was inexperienced and scared.

I looked around for someone who could pray for us. I picked a young man who was a committed Christian and a football player. I'll never forget how he began his prayer. "Lord, You know we are scared to death, but if You will go with us, we'll do this thing for Your glory, Amen." This burly fellow was expressing exactly how I felt. Years later God called him to preach the Gospel. On a visit home from the seminary this young preacher boy said to me, "I've got to go witness because if I let one day go by without sharing the Gospel, the next day is twice as hard to do it." Once again God used him to speak to my heart.

Each team was given tracts to hand out and told to report back at noon. As each team reported back, they shared their experiences. One team returned with news that two people had accepted Christ as their Savior when they shared the tract with them. They were so excited and were anxious to go back out again. They didn't even want to stop for lunch... God used this experience to encourage all of us to continue to be faithful in witnessing and that He would bring the results.

Lessons Learned:

1. When you go in Jesus' name, He will go with you.

2. People are sometimes afraid to do God's will, but He rewards their steps of faith with unexpected results.

3. God works through imperfect people to share the good news so more people can hear the Gospel and be saved.

God's instruction on how to put these lessons to use in our lives:

Jeremiah 1:7-8 (NIV) – But the Lord said to me, "Do not say 'I am only a child.' You must go to everyone I send you to and say whatever I command you. Do not, be afraid of them, for I am with you and will rescue you," declares the Lord.

Acts 1:8 (NIV) – But you will receive power when the Holy Spirit comes on you, and you will be My witnesses in Jerusalem, and in all Judea, and Samaria, and to the ends of the earth.

Mark 16:15 (NIV) – He said to them, "Go into all the world and preach the good news to all creation."

Praying these words back to God.

Almighty God, help us to be courageous while sharing the Gospel because it is the word of life to the world. Thank You for giving us the courage and faith to step out to do Your will even when we are "scared to death". Amen!!!

Lesson Title: Fly Away Home

I used to have a fear of flying…It was very inconvenient since all of my family lived up North and I did some flying connected with my job.

On one of those early trips I was on an airplane sitting by the window over the wing. We were on the tarmac waiting our turn to take off. I'd heard that the most dangerous time when flying was on take-offs and landings so I was sincerely praying for safe travels. I hated sitting there waiting for the mysterious thumps and bumps and engine grindings to begin. I looked out the window and I saw a giant grasshopper sitting on the wing. I watched it as it calmly just sat there. I thought "If you only knew what was about to happen you would just fly away home."

About that time we started moving into position to take off. As we picked up speed going down the runway with the grasshopper along for the ride, it flapped its wings and in a second it was gone. It was as if God was telling me, "If I can take care of a grasshopper, don't you think I can take care of you?"

From that moment on, I have never had any fear of flying. That's not to say that when we hit an unexpected air pocket my arm didn't go out to 'hold the baby in' even though the 'baby' was a forty year old man. Ha!!

I heard of a Father who was concerned about his missionary daughter in Africa during a period of native uprisings. He called her, asking her to come home. "It is too dangerous for you to continue to stay," he said. The daughter answered, "But Dad, I'm in the safest place I could be; I'm in the center of God's Hand."

Once again, God used simple things to teach me lessons.

Lessons Learned:

1. God takes care of us according to His will.

2. Worry and anxious feelings are gone when we trust God's care.

3. Worrying is not trusting God; trusting in God is not worrying.

4. God doesn't want us to be afraid but to calmly trust in Him.

God's instruction on how to put these lessons to use in our lives:

1 Peter 5:7 (NLT) – Give all your worries and cares to God, for He cares about you.

Matthew 6:30 (NTL) – And if God cares so wonderfully for wildflowers that are here today and thrown into the fire tomorrow, He will certainly care for you. Why do you have so little faith?

Philippians 4:6-7 (NLT) – Don't worry about anything; instead, pray about everything. Tell God what you need, and thank Him for all He has done. Then you will experience God's peace, which exceeds anything we can understand. His peace will guard your hearts and minds as you live in Christ Jesus.

2 Timothy 2:7 (NLT) – For God has not given us a spirit of fear and timidity, but of power, love, and self-discipline.

Praying these words back to God.

Dear God, thank You for your loving care of me. Thank You for showing me that if You care for the grasshoppers, I can trust You with my life and that I can be at peace in times of trouble. Amen!!!

Lesson Title: God Is Not Slow

Many people today are wondering why Jesus hasn't come back yet…The world seems like it is in such a mess that surely Jesus is coming soon. But you know, this is not a new question. People in Peter's day were asking the same question, "When is He coming and what are we to do in the meantime?"

God is not governed by time…that is temporal and He is eternal. In 2 Peter 3:8 we are told, "But you must not forget this one thing, dear friends: A day is like a thousand years to the Lord, and a thousand years is like a day." God has promised to return and take His church back to Heaven with Him…. And God keeps His promises.

People are impatient; they get antsy; they worry when things don't go the way they think they should go or when they should happen. "Well, we know God promised to come but He's late!!!" Here is Peter's answer to that silly statement. "The Lord isn't really being slow about His promise, as some people think. No, He is being patient for your sake" (v.9). Oh really? What do you mean by that?

71

"No, He doesn't want anyone to be destroyed, but wants everyone to repent."

So, that's the reason He hasn't come yet. He wants more people to be saved! He is a loving God and He doesn't want anyone to be destroyed. So, He's waiting while more people repent of their sins and come to know Him as their Savior.

Whom do you think this passage is meant for? If God wants people to be saved, who's going to tell them how? Who will tell them about Jesus and the way of salvation? If Jesus came back today, we all know people, even family members, who would be left behind. It would be too late for them to make a decision then....and yet, God is being patient with them and with us by giving us opportunities to share the Good News and for the lost to be saved. So what do we do until He comes? Sounds like we have just been given our marching orders....telling others about Christ so they may be saved while there is still time. Well, what are you waiting for...Go and tell!!!

Lessons Learned:

1. God loves all of His creations even those we don't think deserve it.

2. God uses His people to share the Gospel with the lost.

3. Only the Father knows the day when Jesus returns.

4. We need to be about the Father's business of sharing the Gospel until He comes.

God's instruction on how to put these lessons to use in our lives:

Romans 10:17 (NLT) – So faith comes from hearing, that is, hearing the Good News about Christ.

John 3:16-17 (NLT) – For God loved the world so much that He gave his one and only Son, so that everyone who believes in Him will not perish but have eternal life. God sent His Son in the world not to judge the world, but to save the world through Him.

Matthew 28:18-20 (NLT) – Jesus came and told His disciples, "I have been given all authority in heaven and on earth. Therefore, go and make disciples of all the nations, baptizing them in the name of the Father and the Son and the Holy Spirit. Teach these new disciples to obey all the commands I have given you. And be sure of this: I am with you always, even to the end of the age."

Isaiah 52:7 (NLT) – How beautiful on the mountains are the feet of the messenger who brings good news, the good news of peace and salvation, the news that the God of Israel reigns!

Matthew 24:36 (NLT) – However, no one knows the day or hour when these things will happen, not even the angels in heaven or the Son Himself. Only the Father knows.

Praying these words back to God.

God of everything, thank You for Your patience and Your love for the lost people of this earth. Thank You for delaying Your coming and giving our loved ones an opportunity to be saved. Help us see that it is our job to share the Gospel with our family and friends and strangers along the way before it's too late. Amen!!!

Lesson Title: Jehovah-Rapha

Jehovah-Rapha is one of God's names;
it means "the Lord who heals."

We know that God <u>CAN</u> heal but we don't always know if He <u>WILL</u> heal us or the one we are praying for. We know that God doesn't heal everyone all the time. If He did heal everyone we prayed for...no one would ever die. Someone has said that we should discern the will of God before praying for the sick to be healed.

Why doesn't He heal one and all? There are many reasons that He doesn't heal everyone. We need to pray that His will would be done. So, why doesn't God heal every time:

1.   <u>You have unconfessed sin.</u> (James 5:16, NLT) – Confess your sins to each other and pray for each other so that you may be healed. The earnest prayer of a righteous person has great power and produces wonderful results.

2.   <u>Lack of Faith.</u> (Matthew 9:20-22, NLT) – Just then a woman who had suffered for twelve years with constant bleeding came up behind Him. She touched the fringe of His robe, for she thought, "If I can just touch His robe, I

will be healed." Jesus turned around, and when He saw her He said, "Daughter, be encouraged! Your faith has made you well." And the woman was healed at that moment.

3. <u>Failure To Ask.</u> (John 5:6, NLT) – When Jesus saw him and knew he had been ill for a long time, He asked him, "Would you like to get well?"[7] "I can't, sir," the sick man said, "for I have no one to put me into the pool when the water bubbles up. Someone else always gets there ahead of me."

4. <u>Higher Purpose.</u> (John 11:4, NLT) – But when Jesus heard about it He said, "Lazarus's sickness will not end in death. No, it happened for the glory of God so that the Son of God will receive glory from this."

5. <u>In God's Time</u> (Hebrews 9:27, NLT) – And just as each person is destined to die once and after that comes judgment.

6. <u>Ultimate Healing.</u> (Revelation 21:4, NLT) – "He will wipe every tear from their eyes, and there will be no more

death or sorrow or crying or pain. All these things are gone forever."

Since He knows the future, He knows that if we live, we will suffer more with each day. He wants to save us from that suffering. We know that Heaven awaits those who believe in the saving work of Christ on the cross. Some say it is the ultimate healing to be able to go there.

"God whispers to us in our pleasures, speaks in our conscience, but shouts in our pain; it is His megaphone to rouse a deaf world." – C.S. Lewis, The Problem of Pain

Praying these words back to God.

Dear Lord, Help us to rest in Your hands and trust that You are in control of our days. Strengthen our courage and may we be a testimony to Your loving care. Give us faith to accept Your will when we pray for the healing of our loved ones. Amen!!!

Lesson Title: Spring Has Sprung

Spring has definitely sprung. The beauty of God's world takes my breath away. All of a sudden, the world has gone from grays and browns to yellows, pinks, purples and blues. The pink and white dogwood trees in my backyard are in full bloom, and I can't imagine anything prettier.

There is a tinge of sadness about the dogwood blossoms though, because they remind me of Christ on the cross. There is a legend that says the dogwood tree used to be big and strong like an oak. It was said that the cross on which Jesus died was made out of a dogwood tree and when the tree saw how much Jesus suffered it made the tree very sad. Jesus saw the tree's compassion and told the tree, "No longer will you be upright and tall....you will now be thin-limbed, twisted and unable to be used for a cross." It is said that the flower was given as a reminder. The blossoms are in the form of a cross. The center of the outer edge of each petal is the print of nails. The center of the flower, stained with blood, shows a crown of thorns. Frankly, I don't need a flower blossom to remind me of Christ's sacrificial death on the cross. I am reminded many times of what Christ suffered in my stead.

In fact, there was a time when God gave me a quick glimpse of Jesus on the cross. Not sure if it was a vision, dream or what, but it was a vivid image of Christ on the cross. I was standing at the foot of the cross looking up as He suffered. Jesus saw me standing there and then He looked up into Heaven and cried out, "Father, put Pat's sins on me." That took my breath away....Do you mean that Jesus wasn't there because of the Jews or the Romans? That it was "my sins" that put Him there? When I think of that, I am so humbled and so grateful. Why would He do that? Simply, He wanted to...because He loved us that much!!!

Lessons Learned:

1. God loves us so much.

2. He was a willing sacrifice, dying in our place.

3. God had a plan from the beginning to redeem us from our sins.

4. We deserved death and judgment for our sins but Jesus took our punishment on Himself.

God's instruction on how to put these lessons to use in our lives:

John 3:16 (KJV) – "For God so loved the world that He gave His only begotten Son that whosoever believeth in Him should not perish but have everlasting life."

Romans 6:23 (NIV) – For the wages of sin is death, but the gift of God is eternal life in Christ Jesus our Lord.

2 Corinthians 5:21 (NLT) – For God made Christ, who never sinned, to be the offering for our sin so that we could be made right with God through Christ.

1 Peter 3:18 (NLT) – Christ suffered for our sins once for all time. He never sinned, but He died for sinners to bring you safely home to God. He suffered physical death, but He was raised to life in the Spirit.

Romans 3:22-26 (NLT) – We are made right with God by placing our faith in Jesus Christ. And this is true for everyone who believes, no matter who we are. For everyone has sinned; we all fall short of God's glorious standard. Yet God, in His grace, freely makes us right in

His sight. He did this through Christ Jesus when He freed us from the penalty for our sins. For God presented Jesus as the sacrifice for sin. People are made right with God when they believe that Jesus sacrificed His life, shedding His blood. This sacrifice shows that God was being fair when He held back and did not punish those who sinned in times past, for He was looking ahead and including them in what He would do in this present time. God did this to demonstrate His righteousness, for He Himself is fair and just, and He makes sinners right in His sight when they believe in Jesus.

Praying these words back to God.

Oh, Precious Savior, mere words cannot express my gratefulness to You, O Lord, for loving me and the whole world enough to suffer what You did on the cross. I adore and worship You with all of my heart, mind and soul. Amen!!!

Lesson Title: Dying Testimony

I heard about a mother and daughter who were very close and both were committed Christians. The mother was diagnosed with Stage 4 cancer, and she called her daughter to her bedside and said, *"All my life I've tried to show how a Christian woman lives...now I'm going to show you how a Christian woman dies."* That moved me to tears. God had a lesson in there for me too. I had never thought that the process of dying could be a testimony for others of God's grace.

Her testimony of peace, contentment, and faith during her illness brought some of the medical staff to a saving knowledge of Christ. This woman's dying testimony was one of faith and trust in God, that He knew what He was doing and would be with her until she died and beyond. Heaven awaited her where she would be with Christ for eternity. She had the confidence that the best was yet to come?

If you could control what you said right before you died, what would your last words be? Some famous people have revealed much about their lives by what their last words were:

"All my possessions for a moment of time." – Elizabeth I, Queen of England, d. 1603

"I'm going, but I'm going in the name of the Lord." – Bessie Smith, Blues singer

"D--- it! Don't you dare ask God to help me!" – Actress Joan Crawford yelled at her housekeeper, who was praying as Crawford died.

"I love you Sarah. For all eternity, I love you." – Spoken to his wife. James K. Polk, US President, d. 1849

"I'm bored with it all." – Sir Winston Churchill

"Oh, do not cry - be good children and we will all meet in heaven." – Andrew Jackson, US President, d. 1845

"See in what peace a Christian can die." – Joseph Addison, writer, d. June 17, 1719

"Nothing matters. Nothing matters." – Louis B. Mayer, film producer, d. October 29, 1957

Some died with confidence and hope that they were going to heaven but, sadly, some were still belligerent, hopeless, defiant, and angry, right to the end.

Will my dying testimony glorify God? What will my last words be? I wonder.... Will I lift words of praise to my Lord? Will I tell my family how much I love them? Or will I express words of regret over lost opportunities? Only God knows, but I pray that the words of my "dying testimony" will honor and glorify our Almighty God.

Lessons Learned:

1. Even in death our testimony should be one of faith, courage, and hope.

2. God is with us when we are going through trials and tribulations.

3. God will give us the courage and strength to persevere through our dying experience.

4. Death is a home-going and should not be time of devastating sadness but a time of joyous celebration of a life well lived.

God's instruction on how to put these lessons to use in our lives:

1 Peter 3:15 (KJV) – But sanctify the Lord God in your hearts: and be ready always to give an answer to every

man that asketh you a reason of the hope that is in you with meekness and fear.

Revelation 14:13 (NLT) – And I heard a voice from heaven saying, "Write this down: Blessed are those who die in the Lord from now on. Yes, says the Spirit, they are blessed indeed, for they will rest from their hard work; for their good deeds follow them!"

Psalm 71:15-18 (ESV) – My mouth will tell of Your righteous acts, of Your deeds of salvation all the day, for their number is past my knowledge. With the mighty deeds of the Lord GOD I will come; I will remind them of Your righteousness, Yours alone. O God, from my youth You have taught me, and I still proclaim Your wondrous deeds. So even to old age and gray hairs, O God, do not forsake me, until I proclaim Your might to another generation, Your power to all those to come.

1 Thessalonians 4:13 (NLT) – And now, dear brothers and sisters, we want you to know what will happen to the believers who have died so you will not grieve like people who have no hope.

Psalm 39:7 (NLT) – And so, Lord, where do I put my hope? My only hope is in You.

Psalm 23:4 (KJV) – "Yea, though I walk through the valley of the shadow of death, I will fear no evil: for Thou *art* with me; Thy rod and Thy staff they comfort me."

Praying these words back to God.

Dear Lord and Savior, thank You for the hope and confidence that when we die we will be in Your presence. You said that You were going to prepare a place for us and I believe You. Give me courage and hope as I get older. Thank You for taking the fear of death away. Amen!!

Lesson Title: Who is God to You?

Imagine that you are a missionary and that you have just traveled to the darkest part of Africa... I mean, the part of Africa that has had the least outside contact with the world. You set up camp and begin to settle in for the night. The light from your campfire begins to dim and in the shadows of the forest you begin to see curious faces peering out. The native people begin to emerge from the shadows with crude weapons raised in warning. Everyone from your group is frozen in place, waiting for someone to make a move. You step out with hands raised in what you hope is a peaceful gesture. Someone from your group quickly brings items intended for gifts. You offer them to their leader...and, he, in exchange, offers you something that he has worn around his neck. First contact and no bloodshed...Praise the Lord!!

You are asked through an interpreter why you have come and you answer, "We have come to tell you about our God." Their leader responds, "We have many gods. Who is this God?" You invite the visitors to sit around your campfire and share some of your food with them. How will you answer their leader's question? What would you tell this curious leader about who God is?

By the way, "Who is God to you?" You could do a fill-in-the-blank approach. GOD IS_____.

Lessons Learned:

1. All people have a desire to know more about God.

2. God sends people to tell others about Christ.

3. God will give you the words to say when you go in His name.

God's instruction on how to put these lessons to use in our lives:

Colossians 4:5 (NLT) – Be wise in the way you act toward outsiders; make the most of every opportunity. Let your conversation be always full of grace, seasoned with salt, that you may know how to answer everyone.

Isaiah 51:16 (NIV) – I have put My words in your mouth and covered you with the shadow of My hand – I, who set the heavens in place, who laid the foundations of the earth, and who say to Zion, 'you are My people.'

Psalms 48:14 (NIV) – For this God is our God forever and ever; He will be our guide even to the end.

Psalms 62:7-8 (NIV) – My salvation and my honor depend on God; He is my mighty rock, my refuge. Trust in Him at all times, O people; pour out your hearts to Him, for God is our refuge.

Psalms 68:19-20 (NIV) – Praise be to the Lord, to God our Savior, who daily bears our burdens. Selah. Our God is a God who saves; from the Sovereign Lord comes escape from death.

Psalms 116:5 (NIV) – The Lord is gracious and righteous; our God is full of compassion.

Psalms 54:4 (NIV) – Surely God is my help; the Lord is the one who sustains me.

1 John 4:7-9 (NIV) – Dear friends, let us love one another, for love comes from God. Everyone who loves has been

born of God and knows God. Whoever does not love does not know God, because God is love. This is how God showed His love among us: He sent His one and only Son into the world that we might live through Him.

1 John 4:16 (NIV) – And so we know and rely on the love God has for us. God is love. Whoever lives in love lives in God, and God in him.

Revelation 21:3 (NIV) – And I heard a loud voice from the throne saying, "Now the dwelling of God is with men, and He will live with them. They will be His people, and God Himself will be with them and be their God."

Praying these words back to God.

Dear Father, please give us the opportunity to speak of Your love to others and the courage to do it. We know You will give us the right words to say if we go in Your name. We know that if we take that step of faith You will go before us and make the way straight. Bless Your missionaries and give them souls for their labor. Amen!!!

Lesson Title:
If You do....then, I will....

What is our country coming to? I can't believe the new laws enacted to allow abortions even during labor. I just can't believe any rational human being could think this is right. I pray that even abortion laws will soon be repealed. We've become a nation that seemingly cares more about protecting an eagle's egg than a human being.....

As Christians what can we do to bring about change, to encourage others to return to the God of our beginnings? We pray for our country, but is there more that we can and should do to bring about healing for our nation?

Well, God has a solution to our country's problems, and it is found in the conditional promise of 2 Chronicles 7:14-15:

If My people, who are called by My name, will humble themselves and pray and seek My face and turn from their wicked ways, then will I hear from heaven and will forgive their sin and will heal their land.

Who are "My people, who are called by My name"? That's us...the followers of Christ, the Christian believers, that's you and me. We are told if we do our part then God will do His part.....

What is our part of the promise?

1. Humble ourselves.

2. Pray

3. Seek God's face.

4. Turn from our wicked ways.

Then God says He will do His part:

1. Hear from Heaven.

2. Forgive our sin.

3. Heal our land.

The devil is running rampant. Jesus is coming soon and the devil knows his days are numbered. He must do all the evil he can, while he can. Could it be that our nation is continuing in the state it's in because we, the people who are called by His name, haven't done our part of this promise? God just may be waiting until we are willing to humble ourselves, pray, seek His face, and turn from 'our' wicked ways before He does His part of healing our land and forgiving our sins?

Does God keep His promises?

Yes, He does but the real question is....Do we?

Lessons Learned:

1. Even though our salvation doesn't depend on our "works" there is still work for us to do.

2. God promises us that He will do something just because He loves us (i.e. "I will be with you until the end of the age").

3. God wants us to show a willingness to step out in faith before He shows us His glory.

4. I am asked to make sacrificial changes in my life if I want to have my sins forgiven and bring healing to my country.

God's instruction on how to put these lessons to use in our lives:

Romans 12:2 (ESV) – Do not be conformed to this world, but be transformed by the renewal of your mind, that by testing you may discern what is the will of God, what is good and acceptable and perfect.

James 4:17 (ESV) – So whoever knows the right thing to do and fails to do it, for him it is sin.

1 John 1:9 (ESV) – If we confess our sins, He is faithful and just to forgive us our sins and to cleanse us from all unrighteousness.

Praying these words back to God.

Oh, Lord, please open our eyes to Your will for America. Help us to see what our part is in bringing our nation back to You. Teach me Thy ways, Oh, Lord, and help me to do them while there is still time. Give us divine appointments to share the Gospel with the lost people we see every day. Amen!!!

Lesson Title:
Is Our God Three or One?

I hope you aren't reading this to learn the mystery of the "Trinity" from what I tell you. The word "Trinity" is not even found in the Bible. But God has given me just a glimpse of understanding concerning the Triune God....God, the Father; God, the Son; and God, the Holy Spirit.

God had a lesson for me, in part, about the Three-in-One God. How could that be? My lesson was to have a better understanding of who God is by thinking about my earthly father. My father was a loving father, a faithful son, and a wonderful spiritual influence that is felt even today. God used that simple comparison to help me understand about Him being God, the Father, God the Son, and God the Holy Spirit.

Somehow, I think if we were to see ALL of God all at once, it would blow our minds. We would fall on our faces just like Moses did at the burning bush or like Saul did on the road to Damascus, and like so many others who had encounters with God and were so awed by His Majesty and power that they fell on their faces before Him. So God gives us just a tiny glimpse or two of who He is as we are able to bear it.

I saw an example of God's awesome power one day while leading a Youth Bible Study group in San Antonio. The youth group was divided into teams and sat at round tables set up around the room. They had a Bible Study assignment to read a selection of Scripture, discuss it, and then pray to God about it. The room was buzzing with lively discussions at each table. One by one each team finished their study and then began to pray. All of a sudden I realized that each team was praying at the same time and they were all praying to the same God at the same time...and He was listening to all of them, preparing to answer each one according to His will. That may be a small thing to you, but to me, on that day, God taught me a lesson about how awesome, mighty, and all-powerful He is. I raised four sons, and I know what confusion happens when more than one person tries to tell you something at the same time. I recognized the awesomeness of God who is able to hear and answer each prayer that is prayed every day by all of the Christians around the world.

Can the Creation ever fully understand the Creator? No, I don't think so, but I do know that God wants us to know Him and understand Him better each day and to share that knowledge with others. Is that not the best motivation for missions? Are you still hungry to know more about God? The Bible says, "Seek God and He will be found."

God's instruction on how to put these lessons to use in our lives:

Jeremiah 19:12 (NLT) – In those days when you pray, I will listen. If you look for Me wholeheartedly, you will find Me. I will be found by you, says the Lord.

Deuteronomy 5:4-5 (NIV) – Hear, O Israel: The Lord our God, the Lord is one. Love the Lord your God with all your heart and with all your soul and with all your strength.

Matthew 28:19 (NIV) – Therefore go and make disciples of all nations, baptizing them in the name of the Father and of the Son and of the Holy Spirit, teaching them to obey everything I have commanded you.

Deuteronomy 10:17 (NIV) – For the Lord your God is God of gods and Lord of lords, the great God, mighty and awesome, who shows no partiality and accepts no bribes.

Hebrews 9:14 (ESV) – How much more will the blood of Christ, who through the eternal Spirit offered Himself without blemish to God, purify our conscience from dead works to serve the living God?

John 14:16-17 (ESV) – And I will ask the Father, and He will give you another Helper, to be with you forever, even the Spirit of truth, whom the world cannot receive, because it neither sees Him nor knows Him. You know Him, for He dwells with you and will be in you.

Galatians 4:6 (NIV) – Because you are sons, God sent the Spirit of His Son into our hearts, the Spirit who calls out "Abba, Father."

Praying These Words Back To You.

Our Father, in Heaven, we come to You because who else loves us and cares about us like You do? Only You can answer our prayers. We want to know You better every day. Help us to be willing to sacrifice anything that would get in the way of that. We don't always understand the Scriptures, but we know that You will show us what we need to know each day in Your Word. Amen!!!

■■

Lesson Title: God's Teacup

One of God's most precious gifts to us is a friend. When I lived in San Antonio God gave me a friend named Marcie, who was not only my friend but my mentor. The Bible says a friend loves at all times and this friend did, and she was a gift to me from God.

Marcie was the first person I ever knew who had the gift of hospitality. She ministered to others through her home for God's glory. Many times after church I would get a call from her asking what we were having for lunch. I would tell her what I was fixing and she would say, "Bring it with you and come over." My family of five would go to her house to eat with her five and any other friends or visitors she had invited from church. The house would resound with lively conversations, happy guitar music, and everyone working together to set up tables and get the food cooked and on the table and, 'oh, yes, lots of laughter.'

One day I thought of Marcie and how much she did for other people and I wanted to do something nice for her for a change. I went to the mall and searched for a teacup with a saying about friendship on it. It was hard to find one just right for her because she was so special. I finally found a cup that was so beautiful, and the saying on it seemed to be written especially for her. I bought it and had it wrapped. As I got into my car in the parking lot to go to Marcie's house with my special gift, God stopped me. That's the only way I can express it….God told me that I was to take that cup to a lady that Marcie and I had visited earlier that week to leave information about our church. God spoke to me just as clearly as handwriting on the wall, not in an audible voice but the Holy Spirit's still small voice inside of me.

Well, I didn't want to do it. I had spent over an hour finding just the right cup for Marcie with just the right saying on it, and now God wanted me to give it to a stranger. If you have ever tried to argue with God, you know that you can't win. God's instruction was so strong I knew I had to obey. So, I started the engine and headed to the lady's house. When I arrived at her door, she invited me in. I told her that I had something for her, and she began unwrapping the gift. When she saw the friendship saying on the side of the cup, she started crying. She said that she had been praying that God would send her a friend. We sat down at her kitchen table and had coffee. She smiled as she had coffee in her "special cup." I realized at that moment that it wasn't my teacup, or Marcie's teacup, or even the stranger's teacup, but it was God's teacup. When I left I was so excited to see God in action that I went straight to Marcie's house to tell her that she "almost" had a beautiful teacup. We laughed and rejoiced in what God had done that day. At times like that all we can do is stand in awe of God's amazing plan for each of us.

Lessons Learned:

1. God provides encouragement, love, and fellowship through our friends.

2. God uses us to minister to others in need.

3. God has plans for each of us in His Kingdom's work.

4. Our Spiritual Gifts are used to build up His church.

God's instruction on how to put these lessons to use in our lives:

1 Peter 4:8-10 (ESV) – Above all, keep loving one another earnestly, since love covers a multitude of sins. Show hospitality to one another without grumbling. As each has received a gift, use it to serve one another, as good stewards of God's varied grace.

Proverbs 17:17 (ESV) – A friend loves at all times, and a brother is born for adversity.

Proverbs 27:17 (ESV) – Iron sharpens iron, and one man sharpens another.

John 15:12-15 (ESV) – "This is My commandment, that you love one another as I have loved you. Greater love has no one than this, that someone lay down his life for his friends. You are My friends if you do what I command you. No longer do I call you servants, for the servant does not know what his master is doing, but I have called you friends, for all that I have heard from My Father I have made known to you.

Praying these words back to God.

Thank you, dear Lord, for friends who have loved us and encouraged us to become better Christians. We are so grateful to be a part of Your Kingdom's work. Help us to be more sensitive to Your Holy Spirit's leading. Make us willing to do Your will when we know it. Thank You for allowing us to "see You in action." May we be more like Jesus every day. Amen!!!

Lesson Title: Why me?

The road to Christian maturity is sometimes long and arduous. We grow in small steps...here a little, there a little. I accepted Christ as my Savior when I was ten years old. I am now 79 years old. So I've been on this journey toward spiritual maturity for 69 years. You would think I would have reached the goal and be very mature by now. There have been times of dryness and barrenness in my life but also times of great joy and fruitfulness. I have grown as a believer but I have not reached the point where I can say I have arrived. I believe we continue to grow spiritually all of our lives as we continue to seek Him.

The Bible calls a new believer or an immature Christian a babe. A babe is one who has to be fed on milk instead of the meat of the word. (1) A new Christian or babe in Christ has to be fed and gently cared for. (2) A growing Christian can feed on God's Word for himself. (3) A mature Christian can feed the Word of God to others.

Trials and tribulations come to each of us....As Christians we are not given a free pass from trouble. I have had times of great joy in my life, raising my sons and serving the

Lord in many churches, but my life has certainly not been trouble free. Once something happened that was so horrific that I thought I would die from it. My thoughts at that time were something like this:

"Lord, I have tried to serve You faithfully through the years...why would You allow this to happen to me?"

"This is so horrible that I can't talk about it with anyone."

"I've been a Christian so long I should be able to 'handle' this better."

"Lord, I don't know what to do next."

I was obviously at a point where Romans 8:26 was about to be lived out. "Likewise the Spirit helps us in our weakness. For we do not know what to pray for as we ought but the Spirit Himself intercedes for us with groanings too deep for words."

I thought, as a long-time teacher, I should be able to draw on my experience, knowledge, and maturity to find comfort...I've helped others, why not myself? Not so. I tried to bring forth one of the many Bible verses that I had long ago memorized, but I couldn't remember any except the beginning part of John 3:16, "For God so loved..."; that's all I could remember. I had always loved music and it has been a big part of my spiritual life...so I tried to sing something... Only two partial choruses came to mind, "I love you, Lord, and I lift my voice..." and "Jesus loves me, this I know..."

I was hanging on to my sanity by a very thin thread. Never had I ever been so devastated and speechless before my Lord. That's when the Holy Spirit took over. He showed me that I loved the Lord and that He loved me...and for the time being that knowledge would hold me together until God was able to heal my broken spirit.

As a young Christian sometimes I would question God and say, "Why me?"

As I grew in Christ I would say, "Why not me?"

Later I realized it should be said, "For what purpose, Lord?"

Life does have purpose and it's found in Him…..

Lessons Learned:

1. Growing in Christian maturity involves time spent serving the Lord and proving faithful.

2. Maturity doesn't come all at once; it is here a little, there a little.

3. Joy in serving God is wondrous.

4. God is with you even in the deepest pit of despair.

5. God uses our trials for His Glory to build in us, strength and faith.

6. Our faith is strengthened when we realize God is in control and He cares.

God's instruction on how to put these lessons to use in our lives:

1Corinthians 13:11 (ESV) – When I was a child, I spoke like a child, I thought like a child, I reasoned like a child. When I became a man, I gave up childish ways.

Hebrews 5:12-14 (ESV) – For though by this time you ought to be teachers, you need someone to teach you again the basic principles of the oracles of God. You need milk, not solid food, for everyone who lives on milk is unskilled in the word of righteousness, since he is a child. But solid food is for the mature, for those who have their powers of discernment trained by constant practice to distinguish good from evil.

1 Corinthians 14:20 (ESV) – Brothers, do not be children in your thinking. Be infants in evil, but in your thinking be mature.

James 1:22 (ESV) – But be doers of the word, and not hearers only, deceiving yourselves.

Ephesians 4:11-14 (ESV) – And He gave the apostles, the prophets, the evangelists, the shepherds and teachers, to equip the saints for the work of ministry, for building up the body of Christ, until we all attain to the unity of the faith and of the knowledge of the Son of God, to mature manhood, to the measure of the stature of the fullness of Christ, so that we may no longer be children, tossed to and fro by the waves and carried about by every wind of doctrine, by human cunning, by craftiness in deceitful schemes.

1 Peter 2:2 (ESV) – Like newborn infants, long for the pure spiritual milk, that by it you may grow up into salvation.

Romans 12:2 (ESV) – Do not be conformed to this world, but be transformed by the renewal of your mind, that by testing you may discern what is the will of God, what is good and acceptable and perfect.

Praying These Words Back To God:

My loving Heavenly Father, I love You, Lord, and I know You love me. Thank You so much for that. Help me, Lord, to know and do Your will. May I be more like Christ as I grow up in You. Amen!!!

Lesson Title: Bully Brothers

You know, bullying is so dangerous today. Suicides, injuries, and mental stress, as a result, have definitely gotten the attention of school officials, law enforcement, and parents. It was bad years ago too, but we didn't take it as seriously; at least, I didn't. My solution was to tell my boys, "Just don't pay any attention to the bullies and they will leave you alone." As you can imagine, that went over like a ton of bricks.

One day after school my boys came running into the house and slammed the door, pushing against it to keep someone out. I asked what was going on and they said the Bully Brothers (of course, not their real names.) were after them. They had chased them home from school about 6 blocks away. The Bully Brothers kept up their threats and fights until I thought I needed to step in. After one chase home too many, I invited the Bully Brothers inside. I had planned to reason with them...they were about 10 and 8 years old. I began by saying, "I'm sure your mother wouldn't like it if she knew you were acting like this." The oldest brother defiantly said, "My mother left home 6 months ago, and my Dad said I could beat up anybody that

I wanted to." My heart felt so bad for them. Well, after talking with them a bit, I asked them why they were constantly bullying my sons. Their answer was that they just didn't like them. I suppose that made sense to them but to me it just wasn't a good enough reason to continue tormenting my sons. My sons said that they would get into trouble if they fought them. I told them if they got in trouble for protecting themselves, I would go to the school and defend them. (Rumor had it that my sons were told by their Dad that he would give them $.50 each if they actually punched one of them...Of course, this rumor could not be confirmed.)

My children didn't have perfect parents, but they grew up knowing that they were loved and cared for. Now that my sons are adults, I know they are wonderful sons, husbands, fathers, and grandfathers. They are godly men who love their families and are teaching them to walk in God's way. So sad, that some children do not get the proper upbringing as they grow up. I think the Bully Brothers were seeking attention and getting mostly the negative kind. A little loving care would have gone a long way to keep these two boys on the right track and out of trouble.

I may have missed the opportunity to help them, but I was concerned about my sons and didn't recognize it at the time. I wonder what kind of men the Bully Brothers are today? I guess only God knows.

Lessons Learned:

1. Some children grow up without good parenting and that explains why so many are having troubles.

2. Children who are taught to be kind, to share, and not to fight are sometimes considered weak and are vulnerable to others taking advantage of them.

3. Being a good parent sometimes means we must take a stand against bad behavior in others as well.

4. Some children who are showing bad behaviors are the victims of their parent's poor choices and need loving attention and not harsh treatment.

God's instruction on how to put these lessons to use in our lives:

Ephesians 6:1-3 (NIV) – Children, obey your parents in the Lord, for this is right. "Honor your father and mother," which is the first commandment with a promise – "that it may go well with you and that you may enjoy long life on the earth."

Proverbs 22:7 (NIV) – Train a child in the way he should go, and when he is old he will not turn from it.

Proverbs 29:15 (ESV) – The rod and reproof give wisdom, but a child left to himself brings shame to his mother.

Colossians 3:21 (NIV) – Fathers, do not embitter your children, or they will become discouraged.

1 Thessalonians 2:11-12 (NIV) – For you know that we dealt with each of you as a father deals with his own children, encouraging, comforting, and urging you to live lives worthy of God, who calls you into His kingdom and glory.

Praying These Words Back to God:

Our Most Heavenly Father, we seek Your guidance on how to parent our children. Help us to have godly wisdom in loving and caring for the gifts You have given us. Lord, we look to You for Your protection and provision for our children. Amen!!!

Lesson Title: God's Provisions

In 2015, I felt God calling me to go to Scotland to do mission work. I was 75 years old. Few encouraged me to go, and I realize now that it was because they cared about me and my safety and thought I was too old to travel so far by myself.

I was advised by my pastor to join in with an already organized group. Since there was only one missionary from my denomination in Scotland (who was working with sports), I went with another mission training school. I arrived at my place of service and was welcomed warmly. I was assigned a job in the kitchen as mission support. It was difficult work being on my feet on concrete floors all day, lifting industrial-sized cooking pots, going early... staying late, cooking two meals a day for up to 25-40 people, doing deep cleaning, etc.

I soon became involved in the local church in my free time. Since we didn't have cars or transportation, I walked two miles through the glen each way to go to church and to the Tuesday Ladies Prayer Group. Even though I had planned to stay for the entire year, I was completely worn out in 6 months and began to make plans to come home.

I had lost my confidence for traveling alone. Two of my friends at the school noticed that I had become anxious about traveling home by myself, so they came to me and wanted to pray for me. They put their hands on me and prayed to God, asking Him to provide someone who would help me along the journey and for protection while traveling. They reminded me that God was in control and that I didn't have to worry about it. So my homeward journey began.

The first leg of my journey to Amsterdam began in Glasgow. The young man who sat next to me was a hackney or taxi driver in Edinburgh. He was bent over, and he looked especially weary. I asked if he was okay. He began telling me how tired he was and that he was on his way to a holiday in the Philippines. He asked why I was in Scotland and about my family. When we landed in Amsterdam, he said, "Let me get your overhead luggage down for you, and since I have the time I will just take you on to your gate." God's provision #1. We walked to my gate, and I asked if I could pray for him before I boarded my plane, and he said yes. As I prayed for him and his future, I thanked God for sending an "angel" to help me along the way. I prayed that he would come to know God in a life-changing way. Then I thanked the young man for his help, and as we hugged I saw tears in this rough tough Scottish Lad's eyes. <u>God's provision #2.</u>

The next leg of the journey was from Amsterdam to Atlanta, Georgia. The man who sat in the seat next to me was an engineer from Glasgow who traveled all the time. His wife was a school teacher and couldn't come on his holiday to Arizona for a bicycle trip around the state. I usually cannot sleep next to a stranger while on a plane, but on this ten hour trip I slept like a baby. <u>God's Provision #3.</u> When we landed in Atlanta, the gentleman got my overhead baggage down and pulled out his business card. As he wrote his private cell number on the back he said, "I travel all the time and know my way around. If you have any kind of trouble from this point on, call me and I'll get you the help you need." <u>God's Provision #4.</u> Fortunately I didn't have to call, but it was available had I needed it and that eased my mind.

After landing in Atlanta, the airline had arranged for someone to meet me when I landed to get me to the next gate. A very efficient lady had a wheelchair ready, and off we went. She just took over and wheeled me to get my three pieces of large luggage, took me through Re-Entry Inspections, Immigration and Customs Requirements, and she arranged for several men to help me take my luggage to the last plane. She was one of God's angels. <u>God's Provision #5.</u>

Never will I ever doubt God's loving care and protection during a flight again. He cares and He provides....Thank You, Lord!!

Lessons Learned:

1. God knows what we need before we even ask, and He answers before we even know there is a need.

2. When God does something, He does it right!!!

3. Sensitive Christians respond to the needs of others and they seek to help them.

4. Even in our weakness, God uses us to witness to the lost.

5. God arranges "Divine Appointments" for us as we travel so we can share the Gospel with the lost.

God's instruction on how to put these lessons to use in our lives:

Matthew 28:19-20 (KJV) – Therefore go and make disciples of all nations, baptizing them in the name of the Father and of the Son and of the Holy Spirit, and teaching them to obey everything I have commanded you. And surely I am with you always, to the very end of the age.

Proverbs 3:5 (ESV) – Trust in the Lord with all your heart, and do not lean on your own understanding.

Matthew 7:7-8 (ESV) – Ask, and it will be given to you; seek, and you will find; knock, and it will be opened to you. For everyone who asks receives, and the one who seeks finds, and to the one who knocks it will be opened.

Genesis 28:15 (ESV) – Behold, I am with you and will keep you wherever you go, and will bring you back to this land. For I will not leave you until I have done what I have promised You.

Psalm 46:1 (ESV) – God is our refuge and strength, a very present help in trouble.

Romans 8:28 (ESV) – And we know that for those who love God all things work together for good, for those who are called according to His purpose.

Hebrews 13:2 (NIV) – Do not forget to entertain strangers, for by so doing some people have entertained angels without knowing it.

Psalm 91:11 (ESV) – For He will command His angels concerning you to guard you in all your ways.

Praying these words back to God.

Our most gracious Heavenly Father, thank you for taking such good care of me. Thank You for allowing me to be a part of Your Kingdom's work even in my old age. And especially thank You for getting me safely home from Scotland. Your special angels blessed my heart and did their jobs to perfection. Amen!!!

Lesson Title:
Dumpster Diving for God

Our church has a close relationship with God's people in Guatemala. We've done several medical mission trips and Vacation Bible Schools for the children. God touched the hearts of several doctors who had come with us. The doctors were sad when they did their exams and treatments in places with dirt floors. God touched those men to begin a ministry providing proper health care, and they have since built a wonderful clinic building with all the equipment and supplies. Now the people have more consistent health care and can be treated even though they are so poor.

While on mission there I heard about a lady who lived at the dump. The dump was a place where the refuse from the whole city was brought and just piled up. People would gather when it was time for the trucks to come, and when the trucks dumped their trash they would swarm all over it looking for treasures. They would find items that they could re-sell, food that they could eat, and other things that they could use.

The lady I heard about lived in a house that she had built out of corrugated tin. She had three children, and they lived by sifting through the garbage of hundreds of townspeople. She was a committed Christian. She provided shelter for her family, fed them with the scraps she found, and shared with her neighbors. Once a week she invited her neighbors to her home for a little snack and Bible Study. God spoke to my heart when I heard about her testimony of faith. She had so little, yet she was faithful even beyond her means.

This wonderful lady was such a testimony to me. I felt God was showing me how much I had and how little I was doing with it for His Kingdom. He has blessed me with more than I need, and what am I doing with it to invest in His Kingdom's work? I became more sensitive to needs around me. God gave me a heart for missions when I was a teenager, and ever since then I've been involved in some way or another. Now, instead of going on mission trips myself, perhaps, I will be providing the means for others to go. Thank You, Lord.

Lessons Learned:

1. Going on mission trips puts you on the front lines of serving God.

2. People who go on mission trips experience life-changing events.

3. God uses anyone who is willing to be faithful with what they have.

4. God uses ordinary people in extra-ordinary ways if they are willing.

God's instruction on how to put these lessons to use in our lives:

2 Corinthians 8:2-4 (NIV) – Out of the most severe trial, their overflowing joy and their extreme poverty welled up in rich generosity. For I testify that they gave as much as they were able, and even beyond their ability. Entirely on their own, they urgently pleaded with us for the privilege of sharing in this service to the saints.

Acts 20:35 (ESV) – In all things I have shown you that by working hard in this way we must help the weak and remember the words of the Lord Jesus, how He Himself said, "It is more blessed to give than to receive."

Luke 6:38 (ESV) – Give, and it will be given to you. Good measure, pressed down, shaken together, running over, will be put into your lap. For with the measure you use it will be measured back to you.

1 John 3:17-18 (ESV) – But if anyone has the world's goods and sees his brother in need, yet closes his heart against him, how does God's love abide in him? Little children, let us not love in word or talk but in deed and in truth.

Luke 3:11 (ESV) – And he answered them, "Whoever has two tunics is to share with him who has none, and whoever has food is to do likewise."

Praying these words back to God.

Dear Heavenly Father, Thank You for all of Your provisions for me. Thank You for allowing me to be a part of Your mission to the world. Help me to be more aware of people around me and their needs and how I can help them. Amen!!

Lesson Title: Church on Fire

We were so excited to see Danny, the leader of the local gang, come down the aisle in our church saying he wanted to join. We didn't know that his reason for doing so was to impress one of the girls in our youth group. When she rejected his advances, he showed his true colors. He became very aggressive in berating the members as they came to the services, standing in the yard, yelling obscenities, and going around the neighborhood bragging about being a member of our church. Several deacons tried to counsel him, trying to help him see that he was hurting the church by his behavior. When that didn't work, the recommendation was brought to the church that we withdraw his church membership. I'd never been in a church that did that before, and some of the members felt we shouldn't do it because they thought we could help this young man more if we didn't withdraw his membership. The vote was cast and, sadly, his membership was removed.

Shortly after that, we received a phone call saying that our church was on fire. We quickly ran down there only to watch as it burned. Many of our members thought that it was Danny who started the fire, but without proof nothing was said. We didn't know that his father had given him money that night and said, "Go out and get drunk."

Weeks went by and Danny got into more trouble. He was arrested and had to go to court. Danny's own father wouldn't go with him but one of our deacons who was the local high school principal went down to court with Danny. He was found guilty and the judge was about to sentence him. Our deacon stepped up and said, "Sir, if you will put him in my custody, I will arrange for him to go to a church camp down in South Texas for the time he needs to be incarcerated. We will see that he is housed and fed and that he works hard." The judge agreed.

While Danny was at the camp, God touched his heart and he became a true believer. When his sentence was completed, he came back to our church. Our people were surprised to see him and even more so when during the invitation he came forward. He shared his testimony about how God had saved him and that he was the one who had burned the church and he was sorry. He also said that when the church withdrew his church membership, he realized that this church business was serious. He was welcomed back to the church and forgiven for his actions. God had already done so, but he wanted the church to know the truth. Last I heard, he was an evangelist sharing his testimony of God's amazing grace to him. God is so good to redeem us from our sin.

Lessons Learned:

1. God can and does save people that we think are beyond His saving grace.
2. When we are walking in the Spirit, God shows us how to treat others with love even when they don't deserve it.
3. God gives the faith to step out and do things that are hard to do in His Kingdom.
4. God gives godly men wisdom to help others in trouble.
5. God's will and plan are being worked out in our daily lives.

God's instruction on how to put these lessons to use in our lives.

James 5:19-20 (ESV) – My brothers, if anyone among you wanders from the truth and someone brings him back, let him know that whoever brings back a sinner from his wandering will save his soul from death and will cover a multitude of sins.

Proverbs 11:30 (ESV) – The fruit of the righteous is a tree of life, and whoever captures souls is wise.

Romans 5:8 (ESV) – But God shows his love for us in that while we were still sinners, Christ died for us.

1 Corinthians 9:19-20 (ESV) – For though I am free from all, I have made myself a servant to all, that I might win more of them…I have become all things to all people, that by all means I might save some.

Praying these words back to God.

Our Gracious Lord, thank You for loving us enough to die for us even when we don't deserve it. Thank You for Christians who are willing to help others. Help me to have more desire to win souls for You. Thank You for Your Holy Bible to guide us along the way. Amen!

Lesson Title: Anything Scottish

I don't know why God has given me such a love for anything Scottish. Perhaps He wanted me to go to Scotland and share the Gospel with the Scottish people. I toured the country several years ago and fell in love with the castles, tea rooms, the music, the Isles, and the Scottish people. Many of the well-known Bible scholars, like John Knox, were Scottish. There was a time when Scotland was very religious and many churches and cathedrals were built. Now many of them are no longer active churches. They have been turned into tourist attractions, book stores, and museums. I've heard Scotland referred to as Post-Christian. Many Scots, especially the young people, have turned to other places in their search for meaning. They say, "We've tried religion and it didn't work."

My 75th birthday was spent in Scotland. I was there because I felt God wanted me to spend that year doing mission work. I went there sponsored by a group of people who were already serving the Lord there. I did mission support, which meant I worked in the kitchen. It wasn't what I came to Scotland to do, but I wanted to be willing to do whatever I was asked to do. Much of my time was spent cooking, preparing foods that I hadn't even tasted before, cleaning and trying to accommodate the special diets of the students attending the school.

I did attend the Church of Scotland while I lived in Scotland. On Tuesday, the Church sponsored a community outreach called Rendezvous. People came to visit with other residents in the village and have coffee, tea, and snacks. The Ladies Prayer Group met an hour before Rendezvous. These ladies were concerned women of the church, many of whom were retired missionaries, and also a few from the school I worked in. It was a joy to pray around the world with these Christian women. We had to walk two miles each way through the glen to be able to attend, but it was worth it.

I noticed during our walks to church through the glen that everybody in Scotland seemed to have at least one dog. They were mostly purebreds, and because I have always loved reading about dogs and because I had four sons who loved them as well, I recognized most of the breeds. It became a game with me to see if I could correctly name the breed of the other glen travelers' dogs. God used this knowledge as a conversation starter, and after identifying their dog's breed,I was able to talk with them a bit and invite them to church. It was one of the few occasions I had to witness and I loved it. Who would have guessed that being able to recognize a Hungarian Vizla would be a witnessing tool? Thank You, Lord!!!

Lessons Learned:

1. God prepares us for service by using skills that we don't even know we have.

2. God uses us to help His Kingdom's work even in the kitchen.

3. God opens opportunities to witness in the daily walks of our lives.

4. Churches can reach out to the lost in the community in ways that everyone can be involved in.

5. Even knowing dog breeds can be used to open the way to witness.

God's instruction on how to put these lessons to use in our lives.

Ephesians 5:15-16 (ESV) – Look carefully then how you walk, not as unwise but as wise, making the best use of the time, because the days are evil.

Ephesians 2:10 (ESV) – For we areHhis workmanship, created in Christ Jesus for good works, which God prepared beforehand, that we should walk in them.

Colossians1:10 (ESV) – So as to walk in a manner worthy of the Lord, fully pleasing to Him, bearing fruit in every good work and increasing in the knowledge of God.

Colossians 3:17 (ESV) – And whatever you do, in word or deed, do everything in the name of the Lord Jesus, giving thanks to God the Father through Him.

Philippians 4:13 (ESV) – I can do all things through Him who strengthens me.

Praying these words back to God

Dear Lord, help us to always do Your will. Give us courage to do whatever You ask us to do. Thank You for giving us opportunities to serve You even as we get older. We pray for lost people around the world and in our own country. We pray that You will draw us back to You so we can worship You with all of our beings. Amen!!!

Lesson Title: My Way Failure

It is sometimes hard to know if God wants us to do something or if we are rushing ahead and doing something because we want to. Been there...done that!! My way always fails, but God's way is always successful. One example of rushing ahead occurred during the 70's when God was using coffee house ministries to reach out to the lost. I came up with the idea that our youth would do a "coffee house" at our church and we would invite un-churched youth from the neighborhood to attend. We invited a popular Christian youth band and speaker to come for the night. We decorated our fellowship hall like the inside of a coffee house, including beaded curtains for the doors. We had tables set up with refreshments and special lighting. The days preceding the event we spent hours, and I mean hours, stringing beads for the door curtains. It was fun, and everyone was so excited about the night ahead.

The night arrived, the Band came and set up, the atmosphere was perfect with lighting and table cloths....all we needed now was someone from the community to arrive...We waited and waited but no one came from our neighborhood. We had spent so much time "decorating" that we didn't take the time to invite the lost. My idea...my decorating....my plans...my failure!! God knows our hearts, and He knows that we are weak in some areas of our spiritual growth, and He is willing to forgive us when we rush out on our own, and He will provide the "lessons" for us to learn obedience and submission to His will and way. Please, Lord God, help us in our weakness.

Lessons Learned:

1. Seeking God's Way before doing something saves a lot of wasted time and effort.

2. God's plans are always successful when we obey His direction.

3. God may have approved of the "Coffee House Ministry" in our church, but I didn't seek His guidance, and I definitely did not do it out of concern for the lost. Even though I didn't realize it at the time, I was doing it for my glory and not His.

4. God forgives us when we fail to follow Him, and He is patient and continues to teach us to obey Him in His way.

God's instruction on how to put these lessons to use in our lives.

Proverbs14:12 (ESV) – There is a way that seems right to a man, but its end is the way of death.

2 Corinthians 10:13 (ESV) – No temptation has overtaken you that is not common to man. God is faithful, and He will not let you be tempted beyond your ability, but with the temptation he will also provide the way of escape, that you may be able to endure it.

1 John 1:19 (NIV) – If we confess our sins, He is faithful and just and will forgive us our sins and purify us from all unrighteousness.

Romans 12:2 (ESV) – Do not be conformed to this world, but be transformed by the renewal of your mind, that by testing you may discern what is the will of God, what is good and acceptable and perfect.

Praying these words back to God.

Precious Lord, take my hand and lead me the way I should go. Forgive me when I rush ahead of Your plans. It seems that sometimes I feel I must be drug "kicking and screaming" to do Your will... Please forgive that in me. Give me a greater desire to see the lost come to You as their Savior. Amen!!!

Lesson Title: Precious Possessions

If your house was on fire, what possession would you go back into the house to save? Family albums? Jewelry? Or a pet? As a young adult, my favorite possession was the Bible that my parents gave me on my 16th birthday. My dog even chewed a small corner off of it, but still it remained precious to me. I remember I was in a Sunday School Class when we had a visitor. She was a young Mexican-American mother who obviously had never been in a Protestant church before. When the teacher began the lesson, I realized that our visitor didn't have a Bible to read from, so God told me to give her mine. In my mind I told God that it was my favorite Bible in the whole world...irreplaceable, really... Of course, He knew that already.

I handed my precious Bible to this young woman, knowing that God intended for me to give, not loan, it to her. My smile was a bit weak in doing it, but I did it anyway. Our church lovingly accepted this family into our fellowship and, shortly, this young woman and her family came to know the Lord Jesus as their Savior. God knows what is ahead and we don't, so we must trust that what He wants us to do is good and in line with His will.

I've often said that I've obeyed God many times even though I've gone "kicking and screaming". I know from experience that God wants to bless me and bless others when I step out in faith and do His will. But even knowing that, I sometimes forget and hesitate to move on out. I should know better by now... God is patient with me and teaches me over and over again that when I obey Him, the outcome is always a blessing and always for His glory.

Lessons Learned:

1. God tests us to see if we are willing to submit to His will.

2. God uses us to show His love to the lost.

3. Seekers are drawn to God's people to see if we are sincere before they are willing to hear the Gospel.

4. God is patient with us and will not give up on us even when we give up on ourselves.

5. Earthly possessions have no eternal value except when they are used to draw the lost to Him.

God's instruction on how to put these lessons to use in our lives.

Jeremiah 7:23 (NIV) – Obey Me, and I will be Your God and you will be My people. Walk in all the ways I command you that it may go well with you.

Romans 12:2 (NIV) – Do not conform any longer to the pattern of this world, but be transformed by the renewing of your mind. Then you will be able to test and approve what God's will is—His good, pleasing and perfect will.

John 14:15 (ESV) – If you love Me, you will keep My commandments.

John 1:12 (ESV) – But to all who did receive Him, who believed in His name, He gave the right to become children of God.

2 Timothy 3:16-27 (ESV) – All Scripture is breathed out by God and profitable for teaching, for reproof, for correction, and for training in righteousness, that the man of God may be competent, equipped for every good work.

Praying these words back to God.

Precious Lord, I love You, and I want to obey You. Please help me to love and believe in You more each day. Help me to be willing to obey You even when I am tempted to be selfish and want my own way. Forgive me when I fail to do Your will. I know that I miss the blessing and fail to give You the Glory that is Yours. Amen!!!

THE WAYS OF GOD ARE MYSTERIOUS

The ways of God are mysterious indeed;
Just when I come close to understanding them,
This knowledge seems to fade in and out of existence.
And yet, God Himself is there.

The great I AM is never far from me.
Even though I sometimes skulk away from Him,
Indulging in my anger, resentments, petty hurts, and pride;
Enjoying them until it hurts too much to be away from God.

It's then I realize how lonely I am for Him,
and I come limping back,
Weary from carrying the guilt of sin's momentary pleasure.
Sometimes injured by the world.
Sometimes suffering from self-inflicted wounds,
But always weakened by my absence from God.

All I need to do is take one baby step toward Him and
There, Father God is...
Standing on the porch with outstretched arms,
Welcoming me home.

I would soon lose patience with me if I were Him,
But <u>HE IS</u> the patience of Job.
I would grow tired of me but He loves me still.
Why would He do that???
Because He <u>wants</u> to.

Truly, God's ways are mysterious!!!

"CAN I HELP YOU?"

"I miss her already," she said, as we looked at her teenage daughter lying in the casket.

"Isn't she beautiful?", she asked. We clung to each other and cried.

~~~~~~

Never have I felt the depth of anguish a Mother feels when her child has died, or experienced the anxiety when a phone awakens you with a jolt and you receive the news that , "There's been an accident."

My heart aches when I see others hurting, I feel their pain, but, if the aching pain of others does not move me to act on their behalf…to reach out to them, to touch their hearts with encouragement, to embrace them and cry with them, and to pray for them.. What good is it?

TOUGH ENOUGH

I am not a "hot-house plant."

I have been "hardened off" to endure the long winters of my life. Even now God is "pinching the tops off" of my life to force growth in areas where there are shallow roots and spindling branches.

This helps my roots to grow deeper in Him so that when the dry and difficult times come, I will be alive and strong, tough enough to give shade to others and bear Godly fruit.

OUR KIDS

Wouldn't it be great to always be a hero
to the kids that come our way?
To always hold their attention
with the godly words we say?

It would be nice to have the chance
to help each and every one,
As they come to know the Lord and
serve God's beloved Son.

The truth is, we all have opportunities
to show God's love each day,
When we stoop to touch a life for Christ,
it shows His love in every way.

May we always strive to be faithful
to share God's love and grace,
And our reward will be in Heaven
when we see each little face.

CHERISH THE MOMENTS

(A Tribute to my Dad)

Cherish the times…cherish the places.
Cherish the moments and cherish the faces.
Thinking about them warms up my heart,
And keeps me together while we are apart.

I remember special times at my Daddy's knee,
His wonderful words always come back to me.
He's here in my heart though far, far away.
But I know I'll be with him again one glorious day.

A hand on my shoulder, a touch on my arm,
Strong hands that I knew would keep me from harm.
I knew he was always a man of his word.
He was strong as a lion but gentle as a bird.

Trusting in God is what made him strong.
When we followed his lead, we couldn't go wrong.
Our family is bound with the strong bonds of love,
Like nothing on earth…It comes from above.

God's glory is shared in heaven today
By my Dad who loved us in his special way.
Until we can join him in heaven above,
We'll serve God together with those who we love.

~~~~~

In some Christians' lives,

<u>Christ is present</u>.

In some,

<u>Christ is prominent</u>;

But in others,

<u>Christ is pre-eminent</u>!!

(A sermon outline from the past)

CPSIA information can be obtained
at www.ICGtesting.com
Printed in the USA
BVHW082109021019
560015BV00010B/268/P

9 781787 234086